PENGUIN BOOKS

BAGPIPE MUZAK

Liz Lochhead was born in Motherwell, Lanarkshire, in 1947. She went to Glasgow School of Art to study drawing and painting and there began writing poems, most of which were published in her first collection, *Memo for Spring* (1972). *Islands* (1978) and *The Grimm Sisters* (1981) are included in *Dreaming Frankenstein and Collected Poems* (1984), and *True Confessions and New Clichés* (1985) is a collection of her song lyrics, performance pieces, raps and monologues. Together with *Mary Queen of Scots Got Her Head Chopped Off* and *Dracula* (a radical adaptation of Stoker's classic), both of which are published by Penguin, her other full-length stage plays include *Blood and Ice*, *Same Difference*, *The Big Picture*, *Them Through the Wall* (with Agnes Owens) and a rhyming translation/adaptation of Molière's *Tartuffe*. Her plays for television are *Sweet Nothings*, screened by BBC television in 1984, and *Damages*, still to be produced. She has also written a radio play, *Fancy You Minding That*, and two short stage plays, *Disgusting Objects* and *Shanghaied*, as well as several revues, mainly for Glasgow's Mayfest and the Edinburgh Festival Fringe.

Liz Lochhead lives in Glasgow. She has held several Scottish Arts Council fellowships in creative writing – at Glendon College, Toronto, Duncan of Jordanstone College of Art, Dundee, and Edinburgh University – and has also held an Arts Council of Great Britain fellowship at the Tattenhall Centre, Cheshire. Liz Lochhead was writer in residence at the Royal Shakespeare Company under a bursary from Thames Television. She gives frequent poetry readings in Britain and abroad.

D1113727

LIZ LOCHHEAD

Bagpipe Muzak

PENGUIN BOOKS

PENGUIN BOOKS

Published by the Penguin Group
Penguin Books Ltd, 27 Wrights Lane, London W8 5TZ, England
Penguin Books USA Inc., 375 Hudson Street, New York, New York 10014, USA
Penguin Books Australia Ltd, Ringwood, Victoria, Australia
Penguin Books Canada Ltd, 10 Alcorn Avenue, Toronto, Ontario, Canada M4V 3B2
Penguin Books (NZ) Ltd, 182–190 Wairau Road, Auckland 10, New Zealand

Penguin Books Ltd, Registered Offices: Harmondsworth, Middlesex, England

First published 1991
5 7 9 10 8 6 4

Copyright © Liz Lochhead, 1991
All rights reserved

The moral right of the author has been asserted

Printed in England by Clays Ltd, St Ives plc
Filmset in 10½ on 12½pt Monophoto Bembo

Except in the United States of America, this book is sold subject
to the condition that it shall not, by way of trade or otherwise, be lent,
re-sold, hired out, or otherwise circulated without the publisher's
prior consent in any form of binding or cover other than that in
which it is published and without a similar condition including this
condition being imposed on the subsequent purchaser

In memory of
Margaret Forrest Lochhead
1920—1991

Contents

I
Recitations

II
Characters

III
Poems

I

Recitations

Almost Miss Scotland

The night I
Almost became Miss Scotland,
I caused a big stramash
When I sashayed on in my harristweed heathermix onepiece
And my 'Miss Garthamlock' sash.

I wis six-fit-six, I wis slinky
(Yet nae skinnymalinky) –
My waist was nipped in wi elastic,
My powder and panstick were three inches thick,
Nails? Long, blood-rid and plastic.
So my big smile'd come across, I'd larded oan lipgloss
And my false eyelashes were mink
With a sky blue crescent that was pure iridescent
When I lowered my eyelids to blink.

Well, I wiggled tapselteerie, my heels were that peerie
While a kinna Jimmy Shandish band
Played 'Flower of Scotland' –
But it aw got droont oot wi wolf whistles –
And that's no countin 'For These Are My Mountains'
– See I'd tits like nuclear missiles.

Then this familiar-lukkin felly
I'd seen a loat oan the telly
Interviewed me aboot my hobbies –
I says: Macrame, origami,
Being nice tae my mammy –

(Basically I tellt him a loat o jobbies).
I was givin it that
Aboot my ambition to chat
To handicapped and starvin children from other nations
– How I was certain I'd find
Travel wid broaden my mind
As I fulfilled my Miss Scotland obligations.

Well, I wis in Seventh Heaven
To be in the Final Seven –
But as the Judges retired
To do what was required
And pick the furst, second and thurd
Well, the waiting was murder and it suddenly occurred there
Was something *absurd*
Aboot the hale position
Of being in competition
Wi other burds like masel
Who I should of kennt very well
Were ma sisters (at least under the skin)
Yet fur this dubious prize I'd have scratched oot their eyes
And hoped they'd git *plooks*, so I'd win!
Aye, there wis somethin ridic'lous
Boot sookin in wi thae prickless
Wonders o judges, their 'winks' and their 'nudges'.
Wan wee baldy comedian bloke
Whose jokes were a joke:
Wan heuchter-choochter singer who wis a dead ringer
For a cross between a pig in a tartan poke
And a constipated bubblyjock:
Plus wan wellknown soak –
A member of our Sporting Fraternity
Who was guaranteed his place in Eternity
As a well-pickled former member of the Scotland Squad.
And the likes of them were Acting God,
Being Real Men,
Scoring *us* on a scale of one to ten –

4

They'd compare and contrast, and then at last
They'd deign to pronounce
And reverse-order-announce it.
Then I wid simper, look sweet, an
I'd burst oot greetin
Gasp 'Who me' – the usual story –
They'd plonk me down, stick on the Miss Scotland crown
To crown my crowning glory.

How would *thae guys* like to be a prize –
A cake everybody wanted a slice of –
Have every leering schoolgirl consider them a pearl
Everybody kennt the price of?
How would *they* like their mums to say that their bums
Had always attracted the Ladies' Glances,
And nothing wrang wi it, they'd aye gone alang wi it
And encouraged them to take their chances?
And they were Good Boys, their Mum's Pride & Joys,
Saving it for their Future Wives?
And despite their fame they still steyed at hame
And lived real clean-living lives?

In a blinding flash I saw the hale thing was trash
– I just Saw Rid
And here's whit I did

– Now I'd love to report that I was the sort
To speak out and convince the other lassies
Pick bones wi aw the chaperones
And singlehandedly convert the masses
Till in a bacchanalian Revenge of the Barbie Dolls
Crying 'All for One and One for All!'
We advanced on the stage, full of bloodlust and rage –
But, I cannot tell a lie, the truth is that I
Just stuck on my headsquerr and snuck away oot o therr –
I know I did right, it wisnae contrary –

5

And I let my oaxters grow back in
Really rid and thick and hairy.

Because the theory of feminism's aw very well
But yiv got tae see it fur yirsel
Every individual hus tae realize
Her hale fortune isnae in men's eyes,
Say enough is enough
Away and get stuffed.

Sexual Etiquette

Sexual etiquette,
Sexual etiquette
How to get more of it
And get more out of what you get.

I wonder if you realize
How across this once proud nation
Night-in night-out
There's thousands of women on the receiving end
Of premature ejaculation.

See there's women knowing what they want
But being too shy to mention
So that what ought to be
A fountain of joy
Is more of a bone of contention.

Sexual etiquette,
Sexual etiquette
How to get more of it
And get more out of what you get.

How to ask – very nicely –
Yet sufficiently precisely.

If your husband tends to kiss you
As if you were his auntie,
If he thinks that a clitoris
Is a flowering potted plant, he

Really *needs* sexual etiquette,
Sexual etiquette
How to (a) get more of it
And (b) get more out of what you get.

If he's rolled over and snoring while you're
Screaming 'Not Yet',
If it's a romantic anniversary but he tends to forget,
If he treats you like you're a refugee from 'Auf Wiedersehen
    Pet',
He needs sexual etiquette,
Sexual etiquette.

Advice to Old Lovers

How to be the perfect Old Love. The etiquette?
Well, smile at her a smile that hints at gentle but infinite
    regret
(When you bump into her, years later, at, say, one-of-the-
    old-crowd's 'Big Four O')
Project a certain sense of 'if-you'd-known-then-what-now-
    you-know . . .'
Suggest (wordlessly) that once upon a time you were a lucky
    so-and-so,
Then, when she loved you better than she should of
And you were so mad about her that it was for the good of
Both of you, really, that you split, but – once, oh yes, you
    could of . . .

That should go down well. Well, you know women . . .
Do dance with her by all means. To – e.g. – 'Still Crazy
After All These Years' by Paul Simon and she'll be
    swimming,
I guarantee it, in sentimental, partly alcohol-induced nostalgia
    and hazy
But potent memories of how, together, you were terrific.
Please, though, have the manners to refrain from anything
    too tastelessly *specific*,
Do steer clear of anything that might embarrass
On your little light-and-laughing sorties down Memory
    Lane.
Don't remind her of that night on the hearthrug after 'Last
    Tango in Paris'

Well, nobody wants to go raking all *that* up again.
No apologies. No post-mortems. As Billie Holliday will have
    it: Don't Explain.

No 'I-didn't-mean-to-hurt-yous'. Nothing worse.
If you broke her heart have the grace to imply that, the way
    you remember it, it was quite the reverse.
Some subtler variation on 'We-were- My-God- *wild*-
    together-but-quite-incompatible,
You-drove-me-mad-it-was-impossible!'
That's the line to take. It flatters both,
Is more morale-boosting all round than the truth.

– And gentle ego-stroking's what it's *for*. (You might just
    mention
Her Bloke and Your Wife are getting a touch jealous of the
    attention
You are paying each other, but what the hell –
You always loved each other not wisely but too well . . .)

Don't tell her current Younger Man that she was brilliant at
    the Twist . . .
Do be married to someone who has an even worse record
    than her as a Weight Watchers' Recidivist.
But, please, be Ageing Well yourself, not sad, seedy or pissed,
Or boring, or balding, or wearing a nylon shirt –
To find an old Love *ludicrous*, that's what would hurt!
Well, nobody likes to think they misspent their Misspent
    Youth
With someone they can't-see-what-they-once-saw-in-and-
    that's-the-truth.
The last thing she wants is to see her current love laughing
    up his sleeve –
('*That's* the guy you tried to slit your wrists over? I find that
    hard to believe!
You were six months on Valium? It almost did you in?
That's the guy who Really Made the Coloured Lights Spin?')

No: if your Brief Re-encounter is to be entirely mutually
   delightful and not at all stressful
You ought, really, to be almost (but not quite) as handsome
   and successful
As the Man In Her Life Now, if this can be arranged.
And – if you ever loved her – *tell her she hasn't changed.*

The Complete
Alternative History of the World,
Part One

There was this man alone
In a beautiful garden.
Stark bollock naked
(Scuse my French, beg your pardon)

He was, yes, the original Nature's Gentleman.
He was in tune, at one, with nature
And the lion lay down with the lamb,
Each peaceable creature
Knew its place in the Order of Things
(And if God meant men to be angels
He'd have given them wings).

The climate was brilliant
The weather was sunny
The whole land flowed with
Milk and honey
Soothing fragrant grasses
Waved verdant in the breeze
Breadfruit baked itself in the sun
And fell out of the trees
Where, by the way, songbirds were singing
With bees for a backing
– Oh a right bed of roses!
But there was Something Lacking . . .

He couldny put his finger on it,
He was in a right tizz.
But, the Lord Our God being a Male God,
He knew exactly whit it wis . . .

A slave.

And soon she was worn to a frazzle
Waiting on His Nibs
Ironing his figleaves
Barbecueing his ribs
While home came the hunter
With the Bacon for the table
She was stuck raising Cain
And breastfeeding Abel.
Him: The Big Breid-winner
Her: A Machine for breedin'
Barescud and pregnant?
Some Garden of Eden!
The sort of sexist division of labour
That went out with the Ark –
i.e. the nuclear family –
Bugger that for a Lark.

So they were both Ripe for Revolting
When that Slimy Serpent came
But – would you Adam and Eve it? –
She got the blame.

She could've saved us all a whole lot of trouble if only she'd
told him right at the start:

I'm not your Little Woman
I'm not your Better Half
I'm not your nudge, your snigger
Or your belly laugh.

I'm not Jezebel
And I'm not Delilah
I'm not Mary Magdalen
Or the Virgin Mary either.

Not a Novice or a Nun
Nor a Hooker or a Stripper
Not Super Shirley Conran
Not Jill the Ripper.

No I'm no Scissor-Lady –
I won't snip at your . . . locks.
I'm not a siren, you're not obliged
To get off my rocks.

Not Medusa, not Medea
And, though my tongue may be salty,
I'm not the Delphic sybil –
Or Sybil Fawlty.

I'm not Poison Ivy
You can throw away the lotion
I'm not your Living Doll
I'm not Poetry In Motion.

And if selling Booze and Cars
Involves my body being used, well . . .
I'm not Queen Victoria
But I'm not amused.

And if you don't like my Body
You can sodding well lump it –
I'm not a Tart-with-a-Golden-Heart
Or Thinking Man's Crumpet.

I'm not your Woman of Achievement
Not your Slimmer of the Year
I'm not Princess Diana . . .
No Frog Princes 'ere!

I'm not little Ms Midler
I'm not little Miss Muffet
Make me An Offer I Can't Refuse –
And I'll tell you to stuff it!

'Cos I'm not your Little Woman
I'm not your Lady Wife
I'm not your Old Bag
Or the Love of Your Life –

No, I'm not your Little Woman
Not your Better Half
I'm not your Nudge, your Snigger
Or your Belly Laugh.

Con-densation

After two and a half years with His Mother
We were no longer love's young dream
When me, him and the weans got a hoose o' wur ain
In a four-in-a-block in this scheme.

But – somewhat to our disappointment –
When we turned the key in the door
It was Very Sanderson, very substandard,
When it came to the décor.

Telltale black marks roon the cooker and sink,
Toadstools on the ceiling
And the back bedroom was boggin' wi' damp
(It gave you a clammy feeling).

Plus the bathroom had been invaded
By a sortofa fungussy thing
That looked quite a lot like it was part of a plot
From a horrorbook by Stephen King.

Of course we complained.
We complained again. And – eventually – the Corporation
Sent a couple of fellas who were quick to tell us
'If it's any consolation
The water that's runnin' down your walls
Isn't dampness, it's con-densation.'

'Oh,' says I, 'I see,' says I,
'Whit's that when it's at hame?'
Seems dampness comes in, oot the ootside,
But if it's condensation we're to blame.

Well, taking baths in the bathroom
Or boiling kettles in the kitchenette
Or shutting-up windaes in winter to keep the heat in
Or warming up rooms with paraffin
It all causes steam, don't forget.

Well, pardon us for breathing, (I was really seething)
We complained again. Then complained-again again.
The woman said, 'Now please don't be abusive
I can assure you you've nothing to gain.'

She came she saw she tutted.
She said, 'I see what you mean . . .
Yon's murder on your Laura Ashley
And it's awfully hard to keep clean.'

She was very sympathetic
I have to admit she was *nice*.
But short of hopin' we'd keep the windaes wide open
And the fire oan full blast
And breathe shallow and fast
She was very short of advice.

Well, it's the same the whole world over
It's the poor what gets the blame
And the rich that gets the . . . central heating.
Isn't that a blooming shame?

Well, what do we expect with this Government's
Distribution of wealth –
They wish to get back to Victorian Values
And Dickensian Standards of Health.

The Garden Festival, Glasgow 1988

Garden Festival? I suppose as
Ideas go – well, bread *and* roses
I agree wi' that. I always huv,
But – now we are talkin' here of the City I Love
That, once upon a time, wis a busy place
Wi' muck on its hauns and a durty face.
Well, making things like steel and ships and trains and iron
    meant
A lot of big black buildings and a gey smoky environment
For the loud and proud and bowly legged people of the Clyde.

Yet now 'One hundred acres of riverside
Right in the heart of Glasgow at Princes Dock
Close to the airport and a few minutes' walk
From the city centre with its many fine hotels' –
(Aye, pu' the other wan that's got bells) –
'Is the site of Glasgow Garden Festival Eighty-Eight.
It's fun for all the family' – (I canny wait!)
'It's new! It's healthy! It's educational!
Attracts tourists! Reclaims the Wasteland. It's recreational!
It's a showplace, a get-up-and-go-place', and altogether
We're all all-for-it ('s long's we get the weather).

What is 'a Garden Festival'? Well, it seems,
It's the Glory of the Garden arranged in Seven Themes.
'Today's Garden Festival is the successor
Of the "Great Exhibition" of yesteryear – where as
    possessor

Of an empire you could sell to, showing how great you're
Industry-wise was what it's all about. Today? It's "back to
    nature".'

Oh, I wish I could be sure of a keener re-
Ception for all this greenery,
Could see
Some hope o' a re-
Spite from all this topiary –
Well, jolly japes
Like cutting hedges inty fancy shapes
And trying to make some kinna Eighth Wonder
Oot o' plantin' oot the coat o' arms in floribunda
Are making Scotland just a theme park,
A dream park,
A Disneyland where work disnae exist.
And only tramcaurs
Kelvingrove dinosaurs
And big rusting skeletons of cranes persist
In Memoriam: Our Industrial Base.
It'll cost a packet. It'll be a gey dear green place.
The Garden Festival? I wish we had the courage
To really call a spade a spade and Let Glasgow Flourish.

Festival City:
Yon Time Again

Consider this young, defiantly *un*-Oxbridge playwright
Dreaming of how Stoppard's life was quite transformed by
    Rosencrantz
Last night, OK they had an audience of eight, but really they
    might
Be grateful not to have to toady to mere sycophants!
Theatre, for him, is Language – the what-to-say, the way-to-
    say right
(At the very name of 'Mime' his kekks just squirm with ants)
But what did the *Scotsman* mean: 'attempts both lyrical and
    splenetic'?
Was it entirely a compliment to say 'alternately Brechtian
    and frenetic'?

Mauled by savage critics, the student company pleads
    mitigating factors
(Philistine audiences, the lighting-lady's *minor* faff).
Naff stand-up comics, despite feminist detractors,
Still malign the missus, would slag their grannies for a laugh.
Knackered Veteran Fringe Director/Actors
Long for just a half-hour's kip before the Half.
Wine bars' tills are ringing, and our ears with Theatre Talk
('Jeremy! Jesus, I haven't seen you since Le Coq!')

While Real Year-Round Young Edinburghers sip Camparis
Quaintly – yet familiarly – in some tent.
Demand of each other (in the kind of tone that carries)
Now it's Yon Time again, where last year went?

Once again they meant this year to let the flat and bugger
    off to Paris,
Barcelona (or better) on the proceeds of This Three Weeks'
    Rent –
Except: some horror-commune-theatre-company's drunken
    pukes and shittings
Might prove really ruinous to furniture and fittings.

So, mibbe, in the long run, Being Here is for the best.
They *definitely* are going to go to *something* – once they
    know what's Kosher
And what's Quoted. This year again they tote the diary for
    Bookfest,
Five Official Festival Programmes, the fatter-than-ever Fringe
    Brochure
Plus a confusion of hot-neon handbills and hyping flyers
    pressed,
Like religious tracts, on them by devotees. Yet they're not so
    sure
– Despite flourishing Fringe Sundays and sunnyday floats at
    Opening Parades
Whether the Fringe'll ever be the same post Assembly
    Rooms, post Aids.

A *School* for Scandal? Do we need a school for it?
It's 'Bugger love, give me gossip, I'm a fool for it!'
But whether we need lessons in it I very much doubt –
Unless we need taught to breathe in after we breathe out?
If you're out of sorts, or bored (you know the way)
You'll get a quick lift if you just sift through What the
    Papers Say.
Well, that heady mix of shock and sympathy and moral
    indignation
Will furnish plenty salty details to spice up your
    conversation.
Twice divorced myself, I canny tell you how revived I am
To read how Royal Marriage is a Hollow Sham.

Sunday morning. Your heid's thumping, but you can just
    about handle
A bottle of Irn Bru and some effervescent scandal.
The *News of the Screws* will cure the after-effects of too much
    Glenmorangie
With the Real Life Lives and Loves of Den and Angie.
The Senator and the Starlet – Presidential campaign ends
Once the paparazzi catch them being Just Good Friends.
(Inevitably politicians' financial double deals and lies
Are much less juicy than Sex or Spies.)
The *People*'s journalists are tireless so that all may enjoy
What the Tory MP did to the rent-boy.

Then the *Daily Record* will see you through the week
With an out-of-focus shot of Royals cavorting topless on
    Mustique.
And – in an all colour centrespread exclusive Kiss and Tell –
Rod's ex writes: My Eighteen Months of Hell.
It's Streets of Fear. It's Rape Fiend at Large.
It's Minor Scots Actor on Shoplifting Charge . . .
The bloody scandalrag, yon was very near the bone!
Anyway the case was dismissed, they should leave it alone –
Aye, we may laugh at others, but we get Most Annoyed
If *we* are involved when the shit hits the tabloid . . .

Bagpipe Muzak,
Glasgow 1990

When A. and R. men hit the street
To sign up every second band they meet
Then marketing men will spill out spiel
About how us Glesca folk are really *real*
(Where once they used to fear and pity
These days they glamorize and patronize our city –
Accentwise once they could hear bugger all
That was not low, glottal or guttural,
Now we've 'kudos' incident'ly
And the Patter's street-smart, strictly state-of-the-art,
And our oaths are user-friendly).

It's all go the sandblaster, it's all go Tutti Frutti,
All we want is a wally close with Rennie Mackintosh
    putti.

Malkie Machismo invented a gismo for making whisky oot
    o' girders
He tasted it, came back for mair, and soon he was on to his
    thirders.
Rabbie Burns turned in his grave and dunted Hugh
    MacDiarmid,
Said: It's oor National Thorn, John Barleycorn, but I doot
    we'll ever learn it . . .

It's all go the Rotary Club, it's all go 'The Toast Tae The
    Lassies',

It's all go Holy Willie's Prayer and plunging your dirk in the
   haggis.

Robbie Coltrane flew Caledonian MacBrayne
To Lewis . . . on a Sunday!
Protesting Wee Frees fed him antifreeze
(Why God knows) till he was comatose
And didnae wake up till the Monday.

Aye it's Retro Time for Northern Soul and the whoop and
   the skirl o' the saxes.
All they'll score's more groundglass heroin and venison
   filofaxes.
The rent-boys preen on Buchanan Street, their boas are made
   of vulture,
It's all go the January sales in the Metropolis of Culture.

It's all go the PR campaign and a radical change of image –
Write Saatchi and Saatchi a blank cheque to pay them for
   the damage.

Tam o'Shanter fell asleep
To the sound of fairy laughter
Woke up on the cold-heather hillside
To find it was ten years after
And it's all go (again) the Devolution Debate and pro . . .
   pro . . . proportional representation.
Over pasta and pesto in a Byres Road bistro, Scotland
   declares hersel' a nation.

Margo McDonald spruced up her spouse for thon Govan By-
   Election
The voters they selectit him in a sideyways *left* defection,
The Labour man was awfy hurt, he'd dependit on the X-
   fillers
And the so-and-sos had betrayed him for thirty pieces of
   Sillars!

Once it was no go the SNP, they were sneered at as 'Tory'
    and tartan
And thought to be very little to do with the price of Spam
    in Dumbarton.
Now it's all go the Nationalists, the toast of the folk and the
    famous
– Of Billy Connolly, Muriel Gray and the Auchtermuchty
    Proclaimers.

It's all go L.A. lager, it's all go the Campaign for an
    Assembly,
It's all go Suas Alba and winning ten–nil at Wembley.
Are there separatist dreams in the glens and the schemes?
Well . . . it doesny take Taggart to detect it!
Or to jalouse we hate the Government
And we patently didnae elect it.
So – watch out Margaret Thatcher, and tak' tent Neil
    Kinnock
Or we'll tak' the United Kingdom and brekk it like a
    bannock.

II

Characters

Glasgow's No Different

Hello, my name's Vicki and I'm your waitress for this evening.

And tonight's specials are 'Tagliatelle King Billy', that's a generous dollop of the Pasta Place's *blue* pasta (and remember that real pasta bears as much resemblance to the storecupboard standby stuff as *our* mashed potatoes – nutmeg, cream and a nugget of unsalted creamery butter – does to your mother's packet of Smash). Anyway, 'Tagliatelle King Billy', that's *blue* pasta, a generous swirl of *scarlet* 'al sugo' tomato sauce, a *white* sauce made with wine, cream and garlic and a grating of blue cheese on top. We also do a 'Parkhead Bake' – that's spinach and white fish in alternate Celtic stripes. Evidently Maurice thinks that sectarianism is coming back into fashion as a sort of a Fun Thing. Could be y'know – Maurice is seldom wrong about these things – he's usually got his finger right on the pulse.

Take this place.

D'ye like this place? Well, I suppose yez must, since yez've had to queue up for vernear an hour to get in, and unless this is yer first time here and yer only here to be trendy, then yez've liked it enough to come back. No accountin' for taste, if I didn't work here I wouldn't be seen dead in it. You see, I happen to know what goes on behind those swing doors in that kitchen but it's flavour of the month and the tips are brilliant, so I'm not complaining.

D'ye like the décor? I think that's Maurice's forte really. Him and Gregor, oh that's Maurice's boyfriend and business partner, well they fought over this place something terrible. But I said all along that I thought the Hungry 30s was a great name for a restaurant. It's got that sort of upmarket, cruisin' for kicks sort of ring to it, which is essential if you want to attract the older crowd and that is where all the money is. Not that our clientele are all over thirty of course, but Hungry Over 25s just doesn't have that same Sloany tone to it. Oh, we've got them as well y'know, Glasgow's no different. Maurice calls this design style 'single-end open-plan' and Gregor wanted the place to be called General Strike, but Maurice said 'No! Hungry 30s' and Hungry 30s it is and the rest, as they say, Is History . . .

We did get a write-up in the *Glasgow Herald*'s Trencherman food column. OK, he slagged the food, but he waxed lyrical about the waiters in their galluses, collarless granpa simmets, big tweed bunnets and hobnail miners' boots, plus the waitresses with their neatly rolled hair, crossover peenies and – a lovely wee touch this I think – stockings rolled down to the ankles and Maw Broon slippers . . . So the write-up did help, that plus word-of-mouth, so now on Saturday nights you'll not get a table in here for Love nor Money. Well, not for *money*, but if you happen to be a guy of a certain build and catch Maurice's eye when Gregor isn't looking, then a table just might be found for you . . .

Och, I quite like it in here, really. Well, apart from the other staff, that is. You see, I'm a Professional waitress, MA Honours in History and Politics from Glasgow University, two years in the Ubiquitous Chip. Unlike some. No, I'm not an actress actually. Jesus H. Christ, ever since that Bill Forsyth discovered Claire C. P. Grogan working in the Spaghetti Factory my heart's been roasted wi' the eejits I get working on the next station to me. Skitin' about the flair scalin' gazpacho down the back of some poor guy's new Matinique shirt, can't carry more than three plates at one time – pathetic. Always asking for a lunchtime off or to swap a shift so they can go up and see if their 'agent's got anything' or to go for 'an interview'.

No, they don't call it an audition now, apparently it's only adoring mothers with red patent tap shoes in their handbags taking Lena Zavaroni Mark Two up to the Maryhill Halls for the touring version of 'Annie Get Yer Amazin' Technicolor Jesus Christ Cats Superstar' that call it an audition. This lot call it 'an interview'.

Not that they ever get the job but they're never quite all there here on this job either. Only time they come to life is when some guy from the BBC comes in and then they're practically down on all fours under the table, fighting to be the one to serve him with his Kippers Keir Hardie or Mince and Potatoes John MacLean.

Och, I quite like it really ... Oh, wait till I tell you. This guy came in the other night, dead obnoxious, kept waving this big wad of notes around all the time. Loadsamoney, Loadsa-money – oh, we've got them as well you know, Glasgow's no different. Real case of charisma bypass, I actually felt quite sorry for the poor female that was with him – escort agency written all over her face. Anyway, she orders the smoked salmon straight away, while buggerlugs is swithering over the part on our menu called Soup Kitchen, wondering should he sample the Depression Broth at only £4.50 for a generous brimming plateful and a hunk of bread too, when I suggest the Steak Tartare, and I just knew it ... I only have to pause for breath and in he falls, 'Yes, dear, I'll have the Steak Tartare *medium rare*, please!' The girl and I just look at each other. Of course he's all covered in confusion and blushes after I – ever so sweetly – point out his mistake, and from then on he can't open his mouth without putting his foot in it. Orders a 'cravate of your house white, please'. Then it's 'As you were, as you were, give me a bottle of Chateaubriand.' The girl and I can hardly keep our faces straight, I'm pissing my pants at him up my sleeve ... Anyway, he plumps for the soup and then he complains that 'It's that wee tad on the lukewarm side, dear, d'ye think you could take it back?' 'Oh sorry sir, certainly! Certainly sir,' says I and it's straight through those swing doors into that kitchen and straight into the microwave with it and blast it, I mean, blast it on full. The minute it tings, it's straight through the doors, back onto the table with a clean spoon and just hover about while he touches the plate . . . Y'see the beauty of the microwave is that it heats through the crockery leaving the plate more or less cold. So, he lifts the spoon up to his mouth, in it goes, burns the roof of his mouth, scalds his tongue, sears his epiglottis, he leaps to his feet reaching for the waterjug which I have made quite sure is empty and by this time he's dancing and I just go 'Now, do be careful, sir, it's rather *hot*' and I flounce off to swap gay banter with the camp barman. Terrible really, but you need the wee bijou diversion-ettes, don't you, to pass the time?

Not that you would ever do anything drastic – well, not really – maybe scupper the odd promotion or nip the odd romance in the bud, but nothing to make anyone look a real arse – well not if they're not – but just to encourage them to be all the idiots that they really are. In Public.

But you do need the Ultimate Deterrent though. Not that you would use it – well, not very often, but it's nice to know it's there. Now this is a secret. I shouldn't tell you this. The Princess Di cocktail – now, it's colourless, tasteless, totally undetectable. Y'know Murine? – Murine eye drops? – well, two or three drops into his drink and only as a last resort and if the bugger's been mega-obnoxious, because in ten minutes he'll be going through hoops. Princess Di? – Diarrhoea. He'll be in and out those lavvies for the next two days and I mean *sprinting*. The last time I did it, Maurice comes out the toilets and says 'Yeuch, you should see the state of the gents', and I goes 'Oh, that's a shame – the poor guy could have been taken ill, or taken a dose of salts or something' and Maurice goes 'Salts? Aye, fuckin' somersaults' . . .

So this is definitely the business to be in these days, eh, what with all the tourists and everything? Oh, we've got them as well you know, Glasgow's no different. I'm telling you the Licensed Trades, Restaurateurs and Victuallers Association are blessing the day that bloody Burrell Collection opened its doors. God knows where it is – somewhere on the southside somewhere – well, no bugger can find it anyway, I'll tell you that. There they all are, all those tourists – driving around in their BMWs, looping the loop on the motorway and getting lost over the Kingston Bridge and taking the next exit off and going for something to eat and a wee drink instead.

So, what with Glasgow being a new Cultural Centre for the Arts, and 1990 . . . What with the Opera and the Citz, the Mackintosh and everything, I think it'll be quite wonderful to see all the welders and riveters of yesteryear becoming the waiters of tomorrow. Well, they couldn't be any worse than those bloody actors.

Meeting Norma Nimmo

Hello, hello, it is you, isn't it?

I thought it was.

My, I haven't seen you since school. I have not clepped eyes on you since the Sixth Year Leavers' Social. I mind of you diving around in bleck tights and a big fisherman's jumper shoogling up esperins in Coca-Cola and eating the insides of Vick inhalers trying to get stoned.

You've not changed.

Not really, well, putting on the beef a bit but who hasnae!

Listen . . . listen, do you mind Joyce Kirdie? Mind, reddish hair, freckles, was always a hoot in the French class, did dentistry?

She killed herself.

No, no epperently she wasn't depressed. No, I asked her sister at the funeral, but no, it's a mystery . . . Order in for Liberty curtains, booked up for three weeks in the nice bit of Ibeetha, own Lawrence-home in Kirkie, rubber tube on the exhaust of her H-reg and hallelujah.

Her mother was devastated. Looked about one hundred and five. Mark you, I call it the coward's way out . . .

Do you know who I ren into outside the crematorium? Moira Lennox. Epperently she'd bumped into Merjorie Sneddon. You do mind Merjorie! She won the Mysie Thomson Inglis prize for Excellence in Art three years hard running but wisnae allowed to go to the Art School because her mother was a Plymouth Brethren?

EEC. Brussels. Bilingual private secretary to some bigwig, fabulous selery, she loved the lifestyle. Moira said a week later she was dead, choked on a truffle . . .

Mind you, poor Moira has been having her own share of troubles recently. Ocht, aye you do mind Moira Lennox. Big fet lassie, brilliant at *Letin*. Well, epperently, she joined the Scotstoun branch of the Society of Serious Slimmers and ended up semi-enorexic.

Oh, wait till I tell you . . . Rosamund Petterson. Blondish, right sexpot, used to go out with the Glesgow Ecedemy School Ceptain . . . Modelled briefly. Then she married one of the Everage White Band. Or wis it mibbe the Marmalade? Anyhow, she emigrated with him to Bel Air, he divorced her for Rod Stewart's ex and she ended up with a drug dependency problem living with some elcoholic screen-writer who tried to strengle her to death in a drunken rage. Well, he could efford the good lawyer so he ended up getting off with the ettempted murder charge plus she lost custody of the children.

She's beck home now, running a wee knitwear-and-yarns shop in Clerkston.

Anyway I'm going out with her for a wee G. and T. on Gordie's squash night. She'll be *fes*cinated that I met you . . .

The Redneck

The day I got married I was like a rake.
Six month on the popcorn diet. Starving
but I wouldn't give the girls at work the satisfaction
All so as I could swan down the aisle in my Scarlet
    O'Hara
towards that pig with a knife stuck down his sock.
Kilt suited him, but. Unlike ma da.
A toss-up between the Ancient Buchanan
and the Hunting MacIntyre.
I wanted tartan yes but no too roary.
State I was in everything had to be just so.
I had my mammy roasted in a pinwheel hat.
Ended up whole thing was nothing but a blur
and him shouting 'Perfect Working Order'
every two minutes mooning his mates
and flashing the photographer with his
Lion Rampant boxer shorts. A right rid neck.

During my marriage I ballooned.
None of a family thank God.
Bad enough splitting up without the complications.

Quelques Fleurs

(A Tale of Two Sisters)

One: 19 December

His Mother's a problem. Always hus been. I don't know what she wants.

Take last year, racked my brains, no help from Him as per usual, left to Him we'd end up getting a bottle of Bailey's, a gift voucher and a petted lip all through Christmas dinner! Anyway I done my best, lovely wee lambswool cardi, sortofa mauveish, a *blue*ish mauvey no pinkish, nothing too roary, not my taste but then I'm not seventy-four in February. Gorgeous, but. Self-covered buttons. Scotch Wool Shop as well, none of your made-in-Hong-Kongs. So. I goes into the top drawer of her tallboy looking for clean guest towels for her toilet and there it is. Still done up in the blinking glitterwrap the following November! Says she's keeping it for a special occasion. I felt like saying where do you think you're going, your age, crippled with arthritis? But I bit my tongue.

Thing is too, only the week before – well, He was home at the time, you know, one of His weeks off – and we'd went to the trouble of driving over there and we'd picked her up in the car and we'd took her along with us to my Young Brother's engagement party – uh-huh. Our Steven's settling down at last, my mother's losing her baby – well, anyway we thought His Mother would be company for My Mother while the young ones discoed. Plus it would be a wee night out for her. And naturally it was an occasion for the gladrags, Big Night for the Wee Brother exetra – even Our Joy had made somewhat of an effort. Good appearance, my sister, I'll admit

37

that. If she bothered. I says to her: Listen Joy, I hope you have
not bankrupted yourself paying through the nose to get that
wee costume on tick, I says (because it's a false economy yon
provident cheques and whatnot, you know!). I says: Joy, I'm
sure I could've gave you a loan of something acceptable to put
on. Because since I got myself down to target at the Weight
Watchers we're identical-same dress size, her and me. Peas in a
pod . . .

Anyway I was telling you about His Mother: we get there,
she takes her coat off and, honest-to-God, I could've *wept*.

I says to her, I says, What's up wi your wee lambswool
cardigan, wee brooch on the collar and you'd have been
gorgeous? She says, Och I thought I'd let my hair down, you're
only young once, and she winks at Him. I says to Him
afterwards I says: Your mother. What was she like? Telling
you, talk about mutton dressed as lamb? Crimplene Trousers.
Thon stretchy efforts with the underfoot stirrups. And this
sortofa overblouse affair that quite frankly lukked like it came
from Whateverrys. Big blooming Dallassy shoulder pads, hectic
pattren, *lurex* thread through it, apparently sent away for it out
Myna-Inglis-Next-Door's catalogue, cheap-lukkin wisnae the
word for it. I was quite affronted, you'd think we never
bought her anything decent. I caught Our Steven's Fiancée's
Mother looking at her, eyebrows raised. Although what right
she's got to be so blinking snobbish, all *she* was was a manageress
in Robertson's Rainwear . . . Aye, I think my young brother'll
no have his troubles to seek dealing with that one! Looked to
be the type that likes to *control* everything, get everybody
dancing to *her* tune. Fiancée seemed to be a nice enough lassie.
Pageboy. Good bonestructure, but. Suited it.

I mean, you want to give, but – basically – you want to
give something *acceptable* . . .

So. Our Steven's no problem for once, something-for-
the-house, naturally, what with the forthcoming nuptials, well
they're both *modren* so the electric wok seemed the obvious
thing. *My* Mother's easy pleased, she's had nothing all her life,
give her a good thing she's delighted. With His Mother I give

up. Designer thermals. At least I'll no know if she's wearing them or not! For Him I got the exact same golfing sweater Moira-McVitie-round-the-Crescent-in-the-cul-de-sac got for her man Malcolm last Christmas. Well, He's been threatening to take up golf for yonks and if not . . . well, it would always do for lounging around the house anyway. When He's home. Plus, I've got several wee stocking-fillers for Him, nice wee items in the novelty-line salted away for months hidden at the back of my nightdresses. Well, the July Sales can be a very very good time for Christmas Shopping. Particularly in the discontinued toiletries.

Actually I got Moira's wee minding then as well. We just tend to exchange a wee token thing, just to be neighbourly, nothing pricey – well, what with her Malcolm only being on a teacher's salary I think Moira was frankly quite relieved when I suggested putting a ceiling on it. Because the whole thing can get out of hand. Overcommercialized. Which is a pity.

I hope I done right. I asked Him when He was last home. I said: Country Diary of an Edwardian Lady Drawer Liners, does that say Moira McVitie to you? He goes, *drawer liners*? I said, *don't* start, you know fine well it's for 'fragrant clothes-storage'. He says that sounds like Moira to me. Defin*ate*ly.

So, basically, that just leaves me with the recurring night-mare of Our Joy and family. Because recently I've frequently had the feeling I just cannot do anything right as far as Our Joy is concerned.

I blame My Mother. I mean My Man's God Almighty as far as My Mother sees it. Fair enough. He is a Good Provider, unlike some.

I said to My Mother though, I said: Fair enough you worshipping Him, *fine* you being over the moon we've a new shagpile in the livingroom, but, Mum, I said, there's no need to rub Our Joy's nose in it! Causes resentment. I said: Mum, *think* about it. Use your imagination.

Families, eh? This is the pretty one. This is the clever one . . . Basically Our Joy's always been jealous. Don't like to think that about my own sister but I'm afraid it's true.

Well, of course we're good to the Kids. Me and Him. Naturally. Having the none of a family ourselves. Although Simeon's getting to be a wee shite! Semi-adolescence I suppose . . . Kellymarie, and Kimberly, and that wee monkey Charlene are gorgeous all the same, though Our Joy lets them schlepp about like *toerags*. They're easy! Money, record tokens, clothes, merr money . . . My Little Pony . . .

But that wee new one! Now he *is* a sweetheart. I could *eat him up*, so I could! Went to yon designer-baby shop in Princess Square, yon, you know . . . Kate Greenaway, that imports everything from Milan and France exetra. Got him this, you know, downfilled mini-ski-suit, arm-and-a-leg-time, still it's not every day you become a godmother, all the thanks I got from Our Joy was her sneering at the make: Oh, *Super-bébé*, eh? and turning up her nose at the pattren, which was of Babar the Elephant ski-ing down a hill saying French things in a bubble. Oh, a *ski-suit* eh? goes Our Joy, well, son, that'll come in very handy in Easterhouse! My, that must've cost your Auntie Verena a not-so-small fortune! Which I don't think was a very pleasant remark. Not in response to a gift that was kindly meant, it wasn't . . .

Consequently I've restrained myself Christmas-wise with regard to the baby. *Well*, that was the master-plan, just the matching hat-and-pawkies to complete his ski rigout . . . Un*til* the girl says to me: Have you seen our wee Italian designer dungaree? Just in. I says that's his *name*, she goes what? I says *Justin*, my new wee nephew. Fatal. I can resist everything but temptation, I'm afraid, so basically I'll just have to reconcile myself in advance to another slap-in-the-face from my sister . . .

Her man's no bother. Bottle of Bell's and he's happy. Pleasant enough, mind. Basically a nonentity. Hate to say it about my own sister's husband, but she could've done one helluva lot better for herself than yon. Chances she had. *Her* looks! And smart! All brains, nae bloody common sense . . .

So. Five weans. Man that's no worked since nineteen-canteen. Steys in a three-up in Easterhoose that's that bogging damp the paper's curling aff the walls, has to humph that pram doon three flights past pish, broken gless, auld hypodermics and Alsatian-shite. Excuse my French.

Anyway I thought I'd get her something nice. Something-nice-for-*herself* . . . Upshot, I splashed out over-the-odds at Arnott's, got her a jumbo gift basket. Matching cologne, talc, perfume-crème and body lotion. Gorgeous. 'Quelques Fleurs'.

Two: 6 January

Of course, one year we dispensed with the tree entirely. Tried something I seen in a magazine. Just this barren branch flat-whited with emulsion, *very* sparingly glittered up, you know, just where the twigs forked and just . . . very very sparsely hung with just − mibbe five or six, maximum seven − giant silver mirror-balls. Sort of monochro*matic*. Quite effective, but . . . Depressed me. It wisnae the same.

Moira McVitie came round this morning for a cappuccino. Phoned up and said, Is that your man away back? I says, Uh-huh footloose and fancy free that's me! She says, Yes I *thought* so. Saw you both getting into the car together and I thought that's unusual. I suppose that'll be her driving him into Queen Street for the Aberdeen train? I says, Do you fancy coming round? Sample my new Beverage-Master? Because it even foams the milk. Of course, in the event I spoke too soon and we were reduced to Marvel because I could tell Him till I was blue in the face, but He will be over-lavish with milk in his cereal. Joy can talk though. I've had more black instant than I've had hot dinners round at her house.

So round she came. Wee Scott in tow. I think she's lonely. Says she gets bored, nothing but a two-year-old's conversation every day. I mean he's *lovely*, but he can be quite wearing. Will of his own as well! I said: Do you miss the staffroom? She says: Well . . . I do and I don't. The *banter*, uh-huh.

Usual from her: *I've* got a beautiful house . . . *I've* got

41

marvellous *taste* . . . *hers* is like a *bomb*site but what's the point with young Ghengis Khan scattering his Duplo all over the shop? Wreck of the bloody Hesperus! Plus apparently he's felt-tipped all over her anaglypta . . . says the seven-year-old is *worse*, if anything! Face like a wee angel as well. Goes to ballet . . .

Course, my tree was much admired. I do try and stick to a different theme every Christmas. Obviously this year I'd stuck to two motifs only. I'd Black Watch tartan bows and wee imitation presents wrapped up in Royal Stewart gift-paper. Nothing else. Nothing gaudy, no baubles, no fairy lights. Nothing.

Less is more. We had an English teacher at the school was always saying that. I think it's true.

Course, wee Scotty was into everything what with me being in the middle of dismantling the decorations. Ever noticed how fond mothers tend to just content themselves with the odd don't-son and basically just let the wee buggers run riot?

Moira says to me: I'm full of admiration, she says. See if it was me I doubt I'd bother to go to the effort of a tree. Not if it wasnae for the weans. I don't think that's the attitude. Course I couldny be doing wi pine needles.

Moira says: Did you see that sister of yours on the television? I says, Don't start me. She says: I think she was excellent. Very articulate.

Oh, she's that all right. Always was. Never short of some bloody thing to say, Our Joy . . .

ITV. Some series. 'Frank Exchanges' or some flaming thing. Tale of Two Cities. Joy had to swap wi some other wummin they'd found born the exact same time as her in a private ward in Guy's Hospital, Honourable Felicity something, and they put them through a full twenty-four hours of each other's lives – well, with *limits*, they didny go the lengths of making them shack up wi each other's *husbands* or nothing! Although He blotted his copybook making one or two cracks too minny on that subject to Joy's Man when we had them over for steak pie on the Ne'erday. I says to Him after: You

42

were cruising for a bruising because Joy's Frank has a vicious temper as you well know. When he's roused. Which isn't often, granted.

Anyway this television programme's taken quite a trick with the world and his wife. *Evening Times* called our Joy 'a passionate spokesman for the unemployed, the poor, the polltax rebels'. Said her testimony on the effects to her children's health, happiness, prospects, of living in a damp house in a peripheral housing-scheme of Culture City on supplementary benefit would have brought a lump to the throat of the most hardened Tory. They called her a 'bonny fechter'. I know it off by heart because everybody's been stuffing that blinking cutting down my throat till I'm fed up looking at it – Our Steven, Him, Moira McVitie, Isobel Hislop at the checkout round the delicatessen . . .

Thing is. Our Joy's obsessed with poverty. Makes a meal of it. I mean, I was embarrassed for My Mother. Dragging us up she had nothing, because my feyther – God forgive me speaking ill of the dead – but he'd have took drink through a shitty cloot. But nobody would have known, she kept the three of us beautiful, nobody knew the heartache when wan of us grew out our shoes just when she had the Co dividend earmarked for something else . . . Nae money in her purse to give us our dinner money she'd say: Tell your teacher you've got sangwidges because your mum doesn't have change of a five-pound note! That was My Mother.

And when I saw Joy on that television sitting there on the Honourable Felicity's horse, done up in the breeches, the black coat, the riding hat – they done this bit of filming at a hunt meeting – it was Dorset or Devon or somewhere. In England. The countryside near where the Honourable Felicity's stately whatsit was. Joy said she wasn't afraid of falling off because the sound recordist's assistant actually had it by the bridle. Off camera. And in voice-over she's describing day-to-day in Easterhouse, how you're at the mercy of the medical profession, the social workers, the social security, how the price of taking the kids on the bus into the city centre to go to the pictures was totally prohibitive. Rhyming it all off. No shame. I mean, how did she think My Mother would of felt, watching that?

Funny programme to have on between Christmas and New Year anyway. Not what you'd call festive! Actually it was on the night before Hugmanay among all yon kinna gloomy programmes, you know, résumé of the eighties, lukkin back on all the disasters exetra. Lockerbie. Piper Alpha. You tried to switch channels but they were all at it . . . So Our Joy is quite the celebrity.

Funny thing is, she says she was sorry for that Honourable Felicity, would not cheynge places wi her for all the tea in China. Man's a bad yin, never there, leaving her languishing in the sticks, up at his London flat all week, getting up to all sorts, palling about wi MPs exetra. Stepson a heroin addict.

Course, that'll be how they tracked Joy down for their programme. Be that Mothers Against Drug Abuse thing that Joy is so involved with in Easterhouse.

Aye, she's a volunteer at the Community Flat place, aye campaigning against dampness, sticking up for tenants' rights exetra, single-handed she actually put in for some grant off the EEC. Fought through the red tape and got the funding for pitched roofs and new windows only the shortfall had to be made up by the Housing Department only they said their hands were tied. Blamed Central Government. Anyway Our Joy was up to ninety about the whole thing at the time. Raved on for weeks and weeks. Like I said, she's *obsessed*.

Moira McVitie was saying would I like to join her Book Group seeing I was all on my ownio? Just a few folk she's known since the Uni, couple of lassies she taught with and three likeminded types she met at the playgroup. They all read the same paperback every fortnight, meet in each other's houses to discuss it. Turns out it's at Moira's this Thursday that's why she thought of asking me. Left me a loan of the book they've been reading. I took a wee peek at it over my lunch, but I couldny really be bothered. *Woman at the Edge of Time* or some dampt thing . . .

Anyway that's Him away back this morning. So that's me. Auld claes and parritch! Never really slept right last night, well, you never do.

Och, I hope that's not me heading for another dose of yon honeymoon cystitis . . .

Three: 21 March

Course, I'm used to it now, after all these years, never give it a thought. Well, from the word go, since ever He first went up there on the rigs it's been much better. Definately. Well, financially speaking anyway, I mean see before, with his other job, before, on shore . . . honest to God the mortgage was a millstone.

We first flitted here, I thought we were going to be clomping about on the bare floorboards and sitting on orange boxes watching a wee black-and-white portable for ever.

Him away, the diet is a piece of cake. Well, you've no distractions. Although it is easier now that I'm only on the maintenance anyway. But see when He's home and he gets the munchies and he's up at midnight frying eggs and spattering grease all over my new ceramic hob I could see him far enough – but och well, I just try and tell myself that he's not home for ever, and I bite my tongue.

But you don't tend to bother cooking for yourself, do you? And I am out a lot. Tend to just slurp down a wee cup of slimmasoup while I'm waiting for my carmens to heat up.

Och just round to my mother's basically, just to get out of the house. Although He is that Jealous, vernear divorce proceedings he phones up and I'm no in!

Although as I try to tell My Mother and Our Joy, I'm convinced it's with us having the none of a family ourselves I've adjusted so well. Means I'm a free agent. Moira was just asking me when I was round there the other day, she says: Did you never think to *investigate* it, if that's no too cheeky a question . . .

I says, No, I don't mind telling you, I says, it was a *night*mare Moira, I says, you know nothing about indignity if you've never had your tubes blown.

Doctors! Och it was into the ins-and-outs of everything.

Could find nothing wrong. Nothing wrong with either of the two of us. Not that they could put their finger on. Suggested might simply be missing the moment, what with the two weeks on, two weeks off, mibbe he should think of changing his job, or something?

But och, it's security isn't it . . .

And is a kid compatible with an off-white fitted carpet, that's the question . . .?

Because I gave Moira wee tinkle this morning, asked her round, said she would love to if it was just her, but wee Scotty was having one helluva hiccup with his toilet training.

Hope she wasn't offended I bodyswerved her Book Group . . .

Four: 4 July

I hired a sunbed. Well, you don't want to give yourself a ridneck day one turning up totally paleface at the beach, do you? Although possibly we'll generally use the pool at the hotel, because − if you can trust the brochure − it looks immaculate. Kinna kidneyshape. Although if it's anything like Portugal there'll be a shortage of sunloungers.

So I was saying to Moira if she wanted to come round, because I've the six week hire of the blinking thing, and there might as well be somebody using it. It's not as if I can just lie there all day toasting myself. Over thirty-five and your skin can get yon leathery way. Not attractive.

But she's no turned up. So far. Shame, because it'd help her acne.

Anyway, I suppose we better enjoy this holiday. Him and me, because it'll be our last fling before the joys of parenthood.

Aye, it'll be changed days. Funny how it's all worked out.

It was in the March there, just before Easter anyway. Moira and I went along to see yon Destinastra. Moira had said to me Scotty's wee pal Chloe at the playgroup's mother was having a night in the house where she was getting in a clairvoyant and she was looking for one or two to bring up her numbers. Because with Destinastra it's minimum a dozen before you can get her to come out to you. Moira says apparently she's excellent, prophesied Pauline Patullo would be crossing water for profit in connection with a Leo with the initial R. And here, her husband's boss – *Roy* – turned down the promotion he'd been offered (and had at that point in time accepted!) at head office in Florida because his wife's mother took Parkinson's – so Harry got it and him and Pauline were sold up and off in jigtime. I mean how could she have *knew*?

So we went. Top whack, she reads your palm, does the crystal ball and gives you a choice of either the cards or the Tarot.

She looks at my hand and she says: I see here a secret sadness. I says I don't think so. I says I tend to be quite content with my lot, anyway I don't go around with a long face moaning about things. Unlike some.

She says: No, I can see that you are self-effacing, tendency to sacrifice yourself for others – and was I Taurus? I says no – Gemini – but funnily enough I am frequently taken for one and mibbe it's because I am on the cusp? Anyway, she says I see a Big Joy in your life and it's in connection with the patter of tiny feet. Could it be a sister? Or someone close because it's not actually in your own personal house of happiness, but it's a very, very close-run thing, and will deeply affect you. You and a partner, but I'm not getting him very clearly, is he fairish, anyway that's all very shadowy, am I right to get water, and a brownish car? She said complete change of lifestyle, coming within a nine.

Amazing. And to think that it was the following week before I so much as got wind of Joy's Big News.

Although – and here's where I think you have to believe in something, call it fate, call it what you like – but, this was only days later, Moira had been going down the shops and she said can I bring you back anything, I says och, mibbe the *Woman*. If you're passing. Upshot she brings a *Woman's Own* because it turns out they'd run out – and is there not this big story about surrogate mothers? It's very big in Australia apparently, and they'd two or three case histories, one woman it was her own egg and you know yon in-vitro fertilization with her own husband's sperm and her sister – I think it was mibbe her twin – carried it for her, because there was some blockage or something in her tubes and a badly tilted uterus. Another case, the woman didn't ovulate herself, so her sister (who actually had a grown-up family of her own) had a baby for her, by artificial insemination off the woman's husband. Own husband didny mind, considered it just a case of womb-leasing, a favour one woman could do for another, sister or not and nobody's business but their own. The article took the point of view there were complex issues at stake, legal and financial, and where did you draw the line? Especially where money came into it, was it right to have a child for financial gain, exetra?

So I had been reading that on the Tuesday. Yet when – this was the Wensday – Joy let the cat out of the bag by no means did the penny instantly drop. Far from it.

Well, she was looking hellish, but I didn't think anything of it. Well, I knew she was worried about the poll-tax. That was for starters. I mean it was all very well, but when push comes to shove and the chickens come home to roost they'll seize your television as soon as look at you. All very well these campaigns exetra and those pop stars and well-known celebrities and their Can-Pay-Won't-Pay carry-on. Politicians. I mean it's folk like Our Joy, who've put themselves ineligible for any rebates that are going, or help from the DHSS – basically it's folk like Joy are going to suffer. And I know they've been hounding her recently. Which is a worry.

Plus Joy runs herself ragged all that volunteering and social activating and whatnot she does locally. Newsletters. So it's not unusual to see her looking sorta peely-wally and washed out.

Of course, you've guessed it, it was quite the reverse and she was pregnant! Up to high-do she was, I mean the baby's only what? Nine or ten month old, wee Justin, and when she fell must've been actually still breastfeeding. I says could you not persuade that man of yours to get a job so the time doesny hang so heavy on his hands so to speak? She says very funny. Turns out he'd actually had the vasectomy, but they were still waiting for it actually to be finalized, because it takes a month or two before you can be certain that they're firing blanks, as her GP put it . . . So it was rotten luck.

Thing is as well, she was in two minds. I mean obviously they'd the five kids already, which was more than they'd bargained for because Justin, gorgeous as he is, was a mistake.

But, although the GP said he'd put her in for a termination no question, say the word – thing is, she said, I'm *torn*.

Mibbe it was the fact that – vasectomy exetra – she couldn't change her mind and have another one later, mibbe it was because it felt like slamming the door on her last chance, mibbe it was just that whatever her head thought about it – because definitely they couldn't *have* it – her heart thought different.

My Mother was surprising. She said, Jesus Christ, Joy, get rid of it or you'll never get out the bit.

Joy just sighs and says, I know mammy, I know you're right, OK.

It was driving the car home later that it came to me. Thing is He was due home the next day and I knew I could put it to him. Discuss it. Before I bothered to broach it with Our Joy.

Course in the event the money that we're actually giving her isn't a payment. How could it be, between sisters?

And it's as old as the hills this kind of arrangement, sister for sister, servant for mistress, all through history. Since Bible Days. A lot longer than test tubes or USA palimony lawyers, that's for sure!

No, a friendly arrangement, enough to keep her comfortable while she's carrying – because obviously it's hard work, blossoming or not blossoming! Plus a wee nest-egg for the rest . . .

Five: 24 December

Bought a big bunch of flowers, got myself over there, says where's the labour ward, where do you find the women that have just had their babies, they said Thirteen B, upstairs. Think I knew alreadys, my heart was hammering, tried to tell myself it was just I was just dying to see her. Seven pounds nine ounces. Perfect.

But I knew.

Knew ever since the phone went that morning. Out the blue. No warning. Everything great. I'm driving over there every day feeding the rest of them. Getting mucked in. Three and a half weeks to go. Her totally serene. Blossoming. First thing I knew, he phones me. Her man. Eleven o'clock in the morning and I'm just about to go over for the three girls coming home from the primary for their lunch when he phones me. Says don't bother because he's gave them their dinner money. Thing is Joy went into labour last night at six o'clock and had a wee girl at quarter past midnight. My heart stopped. Says why didn't you phone me. Supposed to let me know. I wanted to be there. He says I know. I know that. Obviously. Just Joy wanted to be on her own. Didny even want *him* there . . . Scratched his face and fought like an animal, doctor hud to ask him to leave because it was upsetting her. I says I'm going in there, he says no, no the now, she's sleeping. Joy is exhausted.

Christmas. No bloody Christmas. Never be Christmas again.

Going to tell Him no to come back either. Go to his mother's. Go wherever the hell he likes. No good to me. Never has been. I-know-it's-a-shock. Big-heartbreak-but-you'll-have-to-snap-out-of-it-sweetheart. Life Must Go On.

Don't care if I never set eyes on him again. He can drill a

big big hole for himself deep at the bottom of the big black North Sea.

And My Mother, coming round here greeting, saying she's sure Our Joy will see sense. Don't want her. Don't want Our Steven or that passremarkable smart-arsed tart he's shacking up with. Fostering. Adoption. Knows fuck all about anything. Any of them. And I told Moira McVitie where to go and take her fat brat with her.

Her. Coming round here crying. Saying she's sorry. Bringing that envelope full of money. I told her I don't care. Tore it up in front of her face. Crying! Trying to touch me, reaching out . . .

Asking me please will I be the godmother. Please. Felicity. Felicity Verena.

Our Joy thinks of nobody but herself. Selfish to the core. God forgive her, because I never will.

III

Poems

After the War

(FOR SUSANNE EHRHARDT)

After the war
was the dull country I was born in.
The night of Stafford Cripps's budget
My dad inhaled the blue haze of one last Capstan
then packed it in.
'You were just months old . . .'
The Berlin airlift.
ATS and REME badges
rattled in our button box.

Were they surprised that everything was different now?
Did it cheese them off that it was just the same
stuck in one room upstairs at my grandma's
jammed against the bars of my cot
with one mended featherstitch jumper drying
among the nappies on the winterdykes,
the puffed and married maroon counterpane
reflected in the swinging mirror of the wardrobe.
Radio plays. Them loving one another
biting pillows
in the dark while I was sleeping.
All the unmarried uncles were restless,
champing at the bit for New Zealand, The Black Country,
    Corby.
My aunties saved up for the New Look.

By International Refugee Year
we had a square green lawn and a twelve-inch tele.

View of Scotland/Love Poem

Down on her hands and knees
at ten at night on Hogmanay,
my mother still giving it elbowgrease
jiffywaving the vinolay. (This is too
ordinary to be nostalgia.) On the kitchen table
a newly opened tin of sockeye salmon.
Though we do not expect anyone,
the slab of black bun,
petticoat-tails fanned out
on bone china.
'Last year it was very quiet . . .'

Mum's got her rollers in with waveset
and her well-pressed good dress
slack across the candlewick upstairs.
Nearly half-ten already and her not shifted!
If we're to even hope to prosper
this midnight must find us
how we would like to be.
A new view of Scotland
with a dangling calendar
is propped under last year's,
ready to take its place.

Darling, it's thirty years since
anybody was able to trick me,
December thirtyfirst, into
'looking into a mirror to see a lassie

wi' as minny heids as days in the year' –
and two already since,
familiar strangers at a party,
we did not know that we were
the happiness we wished each other
when the Bells went, did we?

All over the city
off-licences pull down their shutters.
People make for where they want to be
to bring the new year in.
In highrises and tenements
sunburst clocks tick
on dusted mantelshelves.
Everyone puts on their best spread of plenty
(for to even hope to prosper
this midnight must find us
how we would like to be).
So there's a bottle of sickly liqueur
among the booze in the alcove,
golden crusts on steak pies
like quilts on a double bed.
And this is where we live.
There is no time like the
present for a kiss.

Neckties

Paisleys squirm with spermatozoa.
All yang, no yin. Liberties are peacocks.
Old school types still hide behind their prison bars.
Red braces, jacquards, watermarked brocades
are the most fun a chap can have
in a sober suit.

You know about knots,
could tie, I bet, a bowtie properly
in the dark with your eyes shut, but
we've a diagram hung up
beside the mirror in our bedroom.
Left over right, et cetera . . .
The half or double Windsor,
even that extra fancy one it takes
an extra long tie to pull off successfully.
You know the times a simple schoolboy four-in-hand
will be what's wanted.

I didn't used to be married.
Once neckties were coiled occasional serpents
on the dressing-table by my bed
beside the car-keys and the teetering
temporary leaning towers of change.
They were dangerous nooses on the backs of chairs
or funny fishes in the debris on the floor.
I should have known better.

Picture me away from you
cruising the high streets
under the watchful eyes of shopboys
fingering their limp silks
wondering what would please you.
Watch out, someday I'll bring you back a naked lady,
a painted kipper, maybe a bootlace
dangling from a silver dollar
and matching collarpoints.
You could get away with anything
you're that goodlooking.
Did you like that screenprinted slimjim from Covent
     Garden?

Once I got a beauty in a Cancer Shop
and a sort of forties effort in Oxfam for a song.
Not bad for one dull town.
The dead man's gravy stain wasn't the size of sixpence
and you can hide it behind your crocodile tie pin.

Lucy's Diary *

1

When the big car came for me
I could have sworn I still smelled
my dad's cigar as I leaned back among the leather.
When Jim and the porter sweated to heave
my locked trunk into the back I shrugged
that this was my last time for leaving.
My scorn was all for those
sentimental girls who pressed
keepsake handkerchiefs and cameos and cachou-
boxes into each other's hands and wept and kissed.
I did not look back as we drove off.

Near Birmingham,
red dust, the smoke from my father's factories.
The sunset extra beautiful because polluted.
Dark and a thin, thin moon
by the time we reached seven, the Crescent,
Whitby. Sitting pretty on its cleft cliff.

2

Heartwood is gloomy.
Mama and I quarrel, constantly.
She says I vex her toying with my fork
but imagine if something on your plate

---

*This Lucy is a version of Bram Stoker's Lucy, Dracula's first and perfect victim.

had been a bird once,
well I can't
eat that!
I'll not pick at so much as one feather of flesh,
never. My mother!

Mourning is only a hair brooch
and a heavy dress she will put on.

3

Yesterday
the gardener's big lad
gave me a peach from the greenhouse.
Unthinking, I bit and sucked
then suddenly flung it from me
in a real rage at its beauty.
Something in its furred blush hurt me,
stuck in my throat
like a lump and made me spill,
deliberately,
clouded paint-water all over my watercolour
I'd worked on all morning, spoiling it.

4

I walk and walk and walk.
Florrie says that dog
doesn't know it's born now I'm back.
I wish I were as thin and clean
as that tinkerish boy I caught out today
scudding back with a daft grin –
he must've been all of ten –
from whitecap waves to squirm
into his dirty clothes again.

I'd like to swim far out, not drown.

5

I don't like
the way I look.
I will freckle far too easily, my hair
just won't do the right thing.
When Quincey Morris calls me mighty pretty
it only makes me hate him.

I tilt at
the big, big oval mirror in its mahogany.
This gross flesh I will confine
in the whalebone of my very own
hunger. All term
I would not bleed, not
for Matron, Mama, Mademoiselle,
nor my sister Mina.

6

Despite myself,
the sea air is giving me an appetite.

Renfield's Nurse

When I go in to him
I never know what to expect.
I move in antiseptic corridors.
I come bearing a bedpan like a begging bowl.
I bring hot water, carbolic, huckaback.
I bring a hypodermic, a bowl
of brown stew I've saved for him special,
or three dicey horse pills
rattling like chance in a plastic cup.

Times
he'll be nice as ninepence
sitting up smiling
that pink and bland you'd
swear he'd all his marbles.
Lucid as the next man.

Others
when he doesn't know me from Adam –
though he's always got a glad eye for the girls.
I blame the uniform.

Sometimes
he cowers in his own dirt in the corner
whimpering
Doctor don't you hurt me Doctor.
I say it's just the nurse
I say come on you know it's only me.

He looks up at me
with them dog eyes and says
you the nice one or the nasty 'cause I never
know what to expect?

My hands are gentle.
My starched apron cracks
like a whip hand.

The Bride

I am the absolute spit of Elsa Lanchester.
A ringer for her, honestly,
down to the zigzag of lightning in my frightwig
and it's funny no one, me in-
cluded, ever noticed the resemblance before
because
this fine morning
jolted awake by a crash in the kitchen
the smell of burning
and the corncrake domesticity of dawnchorus toast
getting scraped, suddenly
there's the me in the mirror staring back at me
and me less than amazed at me all marcelled
like Elsa Lanchester.
Well, it's apt enough,
this is my last morning as a
single girl.

Despite your ex-wife's incendiary good wishes,
there's the new frock I've been dieting into for
more than a fortnight
quite intact
over the back of the chair.
And because last night was my last night,
last night I left you,
left you to your own devices under the double duvet
and went home to home-home
to sleep my last night in my own

single bed.
I'd love to say I've my own
old toys around me, et cetera and the same old old-
gold counterpane, but is it likely?
Is it likely what with the old dear's passion
for continuous redecoration,
there's not so much as a Sundayschool prize
not long gone to Oxfam –
just one wall-eyed
teddybear some rugby player gave me for my
twentyfirst
and an acrylic still life with aubergine
(which for one moment I consider asking for –
except where could we hang it?)
to take home to our home, our
old home which today's nuptials must make
our new home,
take home to remind myself of what I can't remember
which is what the hell the girl who did that picture
and was as far as I can remember
painting-daft
has to do with me,
the me with the Lanchester look.

Breakfast.
Breakfast on a tray and like a
condemned man I
can have anything I want for
breakfast, but
before I can lop the top off my boiled egg,
before I can say soldiers far less
dunk them, the place is
bristling with sisters
stripping me and unzipping me
and down the hall the bathroom taps are pounding
Niagara and bubbles.
'Bucks Fizz three fingers cheers kiddo cheerio'

this is Ellen
the older one
the matron of honour
clashing glasses knocking it back
in her slip and stocking soles
plugging in her Carmens
drenching herself in the Dutyfree Diorissimo
Dave brought back from that refresher course in
Brussels with his secretary
unpacking Mothercare plastic carriers
of maximum security sanitary protection from
her Antler overnight case because
she never knows the minute
with that new coil she had fitted after Timothy.
And Susan
our Susan
sixteen, sly eyes and skinny as a wand she's
always fancied you,
ecru and peach, apple green satin she'll
take all the eyes even though it's meant to be
My Day,
the bizzum's in kinks over the under-
crotch buttons of my camiknickers and I'm
to touch nothing till that
Hazel comes to comb out my hair.
Mother is being very mother-
of-the-bride, rushing round squeezing
Euthymol-pink shrimp-flavoured creamcheese
on platters of crackers bigger than millwheels
and though her daughters all agree
a donkey brown twopiece is somewhat
less than festive
at least we're all thankful she's not
drawing squinty seams up the back of her legs
with eyebrow pencil
in memory of her wedding
in nineteen forty-three.

And here's the taxi
and I stretch up my arms
like one beseeching heaven
like one embracing fate
and four sets of hands help me into my dress
my dress I don't want to wear
my dress that after the whole kerfuffle
is really nothing special
my dress that, should you jilt me
leave me in the lurch at the altar of the registry office
tilting my
fragile psyche
for ever permanently agley,
the dress I'll have to wear for ever
till I'm dafter than Miss Havisham
in mourning for my life until it rots under the oxters.
I should have
chosen really carefully.

And then with Dad in the taxi
and I know
it's going to crash because there's got to be
something
going to stop me from ruining my life like this
but no
no Dad winks and one swig
from his hipflask and we're bowling
gaily down the aisle towards you,
you and the best man I've been
knocking off for yonks
with his grin
and the ring
and his pockets
bulging obscenely with apocryphal telegrams.

Because we have opted for a
Quiet Wedding

and a civil sort of civil ceremony
the front four pews are chocabloc with
all our old lovers
who (since we've taken
so long to tie the knot) have all been
married to each other, separated, been
divorced so long
they're on really friendly terms again and
surely someone,
someone will declare some
just impediment to stop this whole ridiculous
charade?
I make my vows
but all the time I'm screaming
'No No No' I
hear a voice
a voice I'm sure I recognize to be my own voice
loud as you like 'I do'.

Despite
the unfortunate business at the
Reception and the
manageress's Jack Russell
depositing that dead rat right at my satin slippers
under the top table while
(animal lovers to a man) the company
applauded laughed and cheered.
Despite
the fact that when we came to cut the cake
it collapsed
like a prizewinning office block
in a spectacular shambles of silver
cardboard Ionic columns and white
plasterboard icing sugar we got
into the going away car while the going
was good and now,
now here we are

alone at last
in the plumbed-in twin-
bedded room of this hotel
where we told the man we'd booked a double
but he smiled shrugged said
he'd no record of that and this was all they had
so take it or leave it.
So we did.

We unpack
our paperbacks. We
scorn such sentiment such institutionalizing as
making love on this our wedding night
and it's only
after (sudden lust
having picked us up by the scruff of the neck and
chucked us into
that familiar whirlpool) and
practised and perfect
we judder totally together
into amazed and wide-eyed calm and
I lie beside you
utterly content that I know for sure
that this is never
ever going to
work.

Papermaker

(FOR JACKI PARRY AT GALLOWGATE STUDIOS)

Rags and flowers perhaps.
What goes into the mulch of memory
is what does not always
grow on trees.

Linen, worn cotton, tattered silk are proper
for the making of fine new paper.
It must have a history
the grind of this hollander
can macerate to what is truly permanent.
Then what pulps, what fluffs of fibres!
Nothing but pure water will gloriously
plump and floss.

What do you love most of all?
Is it the gathering and beating of the fibres?
Or feeling Japanese to be in the morning marshes
gathering cattail-reeds for papermaking,
begging banana-leaf at the botanics,
hanging sheaves of marrams and marshgrasses
from your ceiling like good-cook's herbs
in a giant's kitchen –
singing 'oh I am like the barley
bags of silk'?

The long hairs of inner bark,
the essentials of feather, seed, leaf, grass,
are not like

the industrial slurry of woodpulp and linters
(this too you love:
bleached, maybe,
dyed brilliantly).
Is it best to be more than elbow deep
in the swirled mucilage of the vat
agitating to perfect suspension
every last particle
before you panhandle with your mould and deckle?
Or is it, a minute later,
to know again your own surprising strength
when you, only just, win out against
the dreadful, draining suck
of tonweight water pouring from the mould?
You smile to yourself
satisfied to see a substance
obeying its own laws, cleaving to itself,
every fat fibre loving fibre
when you flip it, single, coherent
brand new on the blanket.
It is like a snowfall,
the first thinnest layer,
almost enough for just one snowball.

What will you make of it?
Rainmaker,
seabeach in a box,
pages from a diary,
wordless books?

Pails of dense dyes,
bowls of pulp.
In the big sink continuous water drips.
Stirred up, the vat reeks of flax dams.
Unshelved
the new Japanese books concertina open
still smelling of kozo, mistumata, gampi.

Good Wood

hardwood
softwood.
sapwood
heartwood.
firewood
dyestuffs coal and amber.
bowls broomhandles platters textile rollers
maple sycamore wildcherry gean.
paperpulp brushbacks besomheads horsejumps
birch.
alder clogs a certain special charcoal
used in the manufacture of gunpowder.
spindles. dogwood skewers.
cricket bats fine willow charcoal for artists' use.
hornbeam oxyokes
mallets cogs and butchers' chopping blocks.
walnut gunstocks
tableware veneered interiors.
poplar and aspen woodwool
chipbaskets matchsticks and matchboxes.
chestnut hop poles posts and stakes.
blackthorn walkingsticks
the traditional shillelagh.
wattle wattlehurdles
peasticks beanrods heathering hazel-withes and hoops.
ash tennis
racquets billiard cues and hockey sticks.
holly for turnery inlaid work and marquetry.

larch planking.
linden hatblocks and pianokeys.
grand fir noble fir douglas fir spruce cypress pine
pitprops paperpulp packing cases
roofing flooring railway sleepers and telegraph poles.
bathtime fragrances of cedarwood and sandalwood.
oak tanning pigmast panelling
and scottish fishing craft.
elmwood coffins in damp earth might warp won't split.

Tupalik

In the museum of anthropology I consider the similarity between the art of the 'tupalik' and the writing of a poem.

What is it?

It is imaginary, magically created.
It is often grotesque.
It is part human, part animal, part sea creature.
It has a bloated belly and its teeth are bared.
It is domestic as dirty dishes,
as ordinary as terror.

Among the Inuit,
where Coca-Cola has rotted the milkteeth of
all the children,
such graven images are often no bigger
than the little finger.

Five Berlin Poems

5th April 1990

Today I got back from Berlin and the broken Wall.
With bits of it.
Smithereens of history, the brittle confetti
of chiselled-off graffiti,
trickle on to the brave blue dogeared cover
of my signed copy of *Sonnets from Scotland*
that I had with me and have just unpacked.
It hasn't travelled well, but crumbled,
this souvenir I brought for Fünfzig Pfennige
picked out from the brightest chips,
from the priciest slabs with names
or obscenities half intact – all on offer
from that grinning gap-toothed Kreuzberg
Gastarbeiter kid who really thought
he had it made.
Well, he saw me coming all right –
another dumbcluck tourist
taking the slow curve of the Wall
towards Mariannenplatz, gawping at
the Bethanien-House artists mending
still-serviceable slogans on what was left standing.
This was a facelift the
chinking chisels of stonepeckers would
only worry at in turn and yet
they painted, and lovingly,
as if these fluorescents and enamels

would last one thousand years
and make good sense.

Every night I spent at Wannsee
at the Writers' House by the Lake,
Morgan's poems whirled me from space
to the bedrock of my own small
and multitudinous country, swung me
through centuries, ages, shifting geologies
till I was dizzy and dreamed
I was in the sands of the desert and the dead
as the poets lived it, just before my time,
then I was following Gerard Manley Hopkins
in priestly black up North Woodside Road
like a taunting Irish boy till I was suddenly,
stone cold sober, contemplating De Quincey
out of his mind in Rottenrow.

And all there was was
the symmetry of these turning pages,
fourteen lines mirroring fourteen lines,
the small circle of light
from the Bauhaus lamp on my borrowed desk
and the sough of trees in the Grunewald.

And outside there was Berlin.
The moneychangers at Zoostation
fanning out fistfuls of Ostmarks,
little lozenges of polystyrene, drifts and
spills from the packaging of dragged
video recorders and ghettoblasters,
blown white as hailstones and as light as popcorn
about their feet.
There was the wasted acreage of the Polish market
beside the Nationalgalerie where
the Ein' Mark, Ein' Mark, Ein' Mark
everything cost was so slow coming in

some of these sellers-in-hell bought
bottles of berry vodka from fellow blackmarketeers
with all they'd made and more, gave up,
got too blitzed to even pretend
to peddle bits of tractor, tools, laces,
mushrooms from polluted fields
bashed tins filched from hungry Warsaw,
bumpy Eastern European school shoes
to the haggling Turkish families from
the U-bahn's Istanbul Express!

And now I'm home
with three painted Polish Easter eggs,
Hungarian opera duets, Romanian symphonies,
an uncopyrighted East German Mickey Mouse
painted the wrong colours,
funny tasting chocolate
and the Rolling Stones 'in ctepeo'
Made in Bulgaria *Made in the Shade.*
And bits of the wall that are almost powder.
I think who could make sense of it?
Morgan could, yes Eddie could, he would.
And that makes me want to try.

aquarium 1

in the fin-
de-siècle gloom
of the berlin aquarium
what little what thick
light we move through (so
slowly) is
underwater green.

lugubrious big fishes
in cross sections of small ponds
bump blunt noses
against their world's end.
there are razorbills, swords, pigsnouts, fronds,
metallics, micas, twists of tiffany glass –
impossible in this changed air to say
what's animal, or vegetable, or mineral.
louvred shoals flicker open shut off on
are gone.
one's a
tilted tin box
articulated awkwardly,
the next is a sinuous slip-of-a-thing
swivelling through tattered café curtains of bladderwrack
with a torchsinger's pout
to a bugeyed audience of
little fish who roll their eyes as if to say
get this
and gasp with just-too-regular-
to-not-be-phoney
openmouthed surprise.

things pulse
like hearts and lungs
in hard-to-look-at
medical programmes on your home aquarium
and anemones bloom and close
in fast photography through
day night day night day night day
five unshrivelling seasons every minute.
here are the lurid tentacles
of amazing latex nineteen-fifties
woolworth's swimming caps.
there is a real
ripper's peasouper
encased in a green glass box

and in it
one obscene frill ripples.

and this, this
is neon graffiti
writing itself, wiping itself
on a wall of water.

aquarium 2

everything
looks more alive
than a crocodile
even the
slimy reptilian turds
of the crocodiles
more likely to slither
or the lumps of terrible meat
nacreous with the iridescent
sickness of the pearl on their
cruel red stumps rejoin and walk
than this shrivelled elbow or
these claws engage not a
splash or even a bubble in this
dire stink you cannot breathe in.
but the ragged long mouths
of the crocodiles and their various
species and snouts
are as indistinguishable and divers
as the sleeping hatreds of europe
and you cannot tell what crocodiles
are made of any more than the
sleeping hatreds of europe

(whether bark or hide or barnacled stone
ancient and primeval and awful)
but these sleeping monuments
are alive and dangerous
as the sleeping hatreds of europe.

three visits

one was eighty seven and hugging john and jane
at tegel then in his big beatup munich car to tadeusz'
open house on schlesische strasse slam bang against the
hard fact of the wall and schlesische tor the end of the line
for gastarbeiters tadeusz' place and the coffeepot that
never emptied kreuzberg kids in and out the trickle of the
wheels of rolf's bike as he brought it in undoing cycle clips
and reaching for a beer and berlin lou reed's berlin belting
out big speakers in berlin by the wall you were five foot
ten inches tall it was very nice candlelight and dubonnet
on ice but it was extra ouzo all round for us at the greek
across the road where any friend of tadeusz was a friend
of the boss and tom and I slept
back in my artschool days it seemed in a borrowed
flat next door where old beaded dresses hung across
the wall in a tangle of bedclothes on the floor newbuild
newbuild newbuild with tom and john and jim arguing
architecture architecture architecture and it was
berlin 750 jahre and the biggest bigdipper in europe
checkpoint charlie where tom was stopped two hours for
carrying in mcniven's tape he wanted us to post in the east
to his musician friend boiled cabbage and you must hang up
coats in the cloakroom in the palace of culture and queue
to go up the fernsehturm to see the whole divided city
spread out below ugly ugly alexanderplatz and die

dreigroschenoper at the berliner ensemble which felt
exactly like the citz death and destruction in detroit
at the schaubühne which didn't and walls came up
enclosed us queenie lying on the floor four hours long the
play and her belly huge two weeks before louisa we stayed
up all night dancing and took the plane home reeling drunk.

two was george wylie a bird is not a stone a christmas
schoolkids' sculpture project at the wall schmuck and trees
glühwein and sugared cookies in the cold cold glittering
square around gedächtniskirche ka de we brandied fruits
like jewels jewels like brandied fruits frozen wannsee
to friedrichstrasse and duty free whisky to take to the east
   berlin
poetry reading in the pottery where the wheel turned and
the poets were illegal and it was nearly the darkest day of the
year the first snow of winter nineteen eighty eight.

three was after the wall was opened and one single city
amazed
and bursting at the seams in nineteen ninety

Almost-Christmas at the Writers' House

   Morgan, master of the Instamatic Poem,
   has flung open the glass door
   – three storeys up –
   of this high guest suite, and,
   his own camera cocked and ready,
   flashgun primed,
   is muttering 'Mag-ritte, Mag-grrritte'
   with a mock-burr and much glee.
   About to freeze-frame the scene before him.

Untouched by even a spring of birdclaw,
perfect behind wrought-iron battlements,
twenty or thirty feet of
snowy rooftop
sports a chair and round terrazzo-table
tipsily iced with an inches-deep drift.
Directly opposite
behind another rooftop door
which mirrors this,
lit up by slicing beams of anglepoise
but quite, quite empty this late at night
is the beautiful Bauhaus calm
of the office of the director of the
Literarisches Colloquium.

Behind Morgan,
Withers, Mulrine, McNaughtan, Lochhead,
well-clad, scarved and booted
stamp and laugh
(impatient for Gulaschsuppe and Berliner Weisse
at the restaurant by Wannsee S. Bahnhof)
then breathe, stilled
as his shutter falls, stopped
by this one moment's
crystalline unbroken vision
of the dreaming order in the
purring electric heart of the house of our hosts.

READ MORE IN PENGUIN

In every corner of the world, on every subject under the sun, Penguin represents quality and variety – the very best in publishing today.

For complete information about books available from Penguin – including Puffins, Penguin Classics and Arkana – and how to order them, write to us at the appropriate address below. Please note that for copyright reasons the selection of books varies from country to country.

In the United Kingdom: Please write to *Dept. JC, Penguin Books Ltd, FREEPOST, West Drayton, Middlesex UB7 OBR.*

If you have any difficulty in obtaining a title, please send your order with the correct money, plus ten per cent for postage and packaging, to *PO Box No. 11, West Drayton, Middlesex UB7 OBR*

In the United States: Please write to *Consumer Sales, Penguin USA, P.O. Box 999, Dept. 17109, Bergenfield, New Jersey 07621-0120.* VISA and MasterCard holders call 1-800-253-6476 to order all Penguin titles

In Canada: Please write to *Penguin Books Canada Ltd, 10 Alcorn Avenue, Suite 300, Toronto, Ontario M4V 3B2*

In Australia: Please write to *Penguin Books Australia Ltd, P.O. Box 257, Ringwood, Victoria 3134*

In New Zealand: Please write to *Penguin Books (NZ) Ltd, Private Bag 102902, North Shore Mail Centre, Auckland 10*

In India: Please write to *Penguin Books India Pvt Ltd, 706 Eros Apartments, 56 Nehru Place, New Delhi 110 019*

In the Netherlands: Please write to *Penguin Books Netherlands bv, Postbus 3507, NL-1001 AH Amsterdam*

In Germany: Please write to *Penguin Books Deutschland GmbH, Metzlerstrasse 26, 60594 Frankfurt am Main*

In Spain: Please write to *Penguin Books S. A., Bravo Murillo 19, 1° B, 28015 Madrid*

In Italy: Please write to *Penguin Italia s.r.l., Via Felice Casati 20, I–20124 Milano*

In France: Please write to *Penguin France S. A., 17 rue Lejeune, F–31000 Toulouse*

In Japan: Please write to *Penguin Books Japan, Ishikiribashi Building, 2–5–4, Suido, Bunkyo-ku, Tokyo 112*

In Greece: Please write to *Penguin Hellas Ltd, Dimocritou 3, GR–106 71 Athens*

In South Africa: Please write to *Longman Penguin Southern Africa (Pty) Ltd, Private Bag X08, Bertsham 2013*

BY THE SAME AUTHOR

Mary Queen of Scots Got Her Head Chopped Off and **Dracula**

'It draws the most dramatic and uncomfortable parallels between the sacrifice of Mary in her day, and the myriad sexual, political and religious deformities that still plague the Scottish psyche ... a play that blasts Mary's myths not out of mindless radicalism, but because it has something more important to say about her and about us, about womanhood and the nation' – *Guardian*

'Liz Lochhead's *Dracula* shrugs off all those fanged Hammer spoofs and restores real tragedy to Bram Stoker's tale ... In this powerful and poetic vision ... Lochhead moves beyond Stoker too. The outpourings of a madman paradoxically reveal the sort of sanity Lear's Fool supplied and he becomes, in his chains and straitjacket, an image of the chaotic unacceptable truth within us all' – *Guardian*

Mary Queen of Scots Got Her Head Chopped Off won an Edinburgh Festival Fringe First